Awkward Angel

SHANNON GOWENS

To order additional copies of this book, contact:
Xlibris
844-714-8691
www.Xlibris.com
Orders@Xlibris.com

ISBN: Softcover   978-1-6641-6503-8
         EBook   978-1-6641-6502-1

Print information available on the last page

Rev. date: 04/08/2021

Sweet love
My heart
I am such a fool
To believe I have it encased in maturity
Protected by experience and discipline
It is not mine to command
It reaches without arms
Like gravity - at odds with practicality
Senseless
Helpless
I am judged, vulnerable, confused
Conflicted but with you
Aware of every skin cell, hair follicle
I feel my eye lashes like butterfly wings and the space between my lips and teeth
I could kiss your skin for hours
And look into your eyes for days

When hearts break
What do we do when a heart breaks?
It depends-
Did you cause it or steer it that way
Even unintentionally, you bare burden
Boulders or pebbles - subjective, perspective
The view varies between pairing eyes
And pleads innocent intentions
Perhaps fault without focus
Or focus without conscious intention
or the deep lies we tell ourselves to sleep at night
You're innocent - sleep tight
Or is it complex - Complicated
Mixed and twisted
Like ribbons on a May Day pole
Or school girls practicing braids
Fat layers, bunching over wisps - lumps and lopsided
Lovers shouting 'their' wrongs and 'my' rights high on familiar towers of praise and parroting
Sometimes seemingly endless bellows of testimony
Trying to prove a rain cloud, wave crest, or summer season was theirs
Or was it blind
Unexpected
The kind that exhales your heart into your stomach - freezes you slightly hunched over
Unable to look at anything but the floor
That causes you to wince at a thousand photographs - a thousand memories
Fools love
Consider - the previous two heart breaks discussed here - with time, always heal
Through talking, folding, molding, stretching, stroking the wounds
The last way
Never does

Delicate

Delicate, but not really fragile
Soft, but won't yield to every touch
Kind, but not easily broken
She holds her ground despite underestimation
Sometimes her underestimation
Lacking confidence in theory, but her body knows better
Her ancestors knew better
Her veins, her blood, her organs and skin
Hold knowledge she doesn't trust
If she would stop thinking
Her bones would tell her the truth

I still love you
But I won't tell you
Because it doesn't matter
Or change anything
But to say I don't would be a lie
I don't want to
I'm smart and practical in most things
But no matter what you say or do to me
I can't

A kiss

Long discussed and considered

Often built up to a monumental let down

Disappointment

Fast and eager

I would have understood - weeks to months of dialogue and fantasy

Without promise or consistent interest

The worst kind of interest in fact

Transient

Noncommittal

Indifferent

Truly shameful disinterest. Not wanting to admit it

Until - a kiss

The kind that lingers in your brain

And digs in with nails

You will never touch me again
You will never touch me again
Not a hug, or hand hold
Shoulder touch or brush
Your lips will never touch mine - and I struggle to remember the last kiss
If it was memorable
Ah! Now I remember
It wasn't - you weren't
My punishment is also yours
For you will never feel my skin
Or tilt my chin
Or hold my gaze - or my trust
You will never again melt my heart
Never again

Broken

Splintered, heartache, painful

Life has a way of being life - heavy

Some carry more weight

Some - like balls to juggle - various shapes and sizes

Almost impossible to prepare and brace for,

Shield against weather and harsh elements

Temperate - unforgiving sun

◦ But that skin is rough and rubbed raw

◦ Doesn't reflect her core

◦ She fears she has lost something

◦ Some part of herself through these burning and butchering lessons

◦ But she doesn't see - what we see - I see

◦ What we love is still there - never changes

◦ That flame flickers with fear - sadness

◦ But never dies

Clawing at emotion
I think of you and have to distance myself
What's your interest? My investment?
I want your hands on me always
To feel your kindness and not your cold shoulder
I see you
I know you
And I don't buy your bravado
But I have to protect myself too
Love sometimes isn't enough
And yet, I'm still here

I hate you

All of you - the people who read my texts and don't respond

Or ignore my voicemails entirely

Wait all day simply to make an excuse

To avoid

To fabricate

To behave cowardly

I hate you

But that's only because I love you

I asked for you
You came
And I laughed at the irony
And found the curiosity humorous
And I enjoyed the sarcasm of the moment
Clearly a cosmic joke
Poking fun at my request
I was prepared to accept it
Like a shallow gift - from a distant aunt - crystal vase or neutral linen sheets
But you spoke - took time and were thoughtful
Careful in your response
Spent hours unraveling - unexpected layers
I attacked - venom and armor
You
You aren't supposed to exist - I'm angry at the complexity
That it's possible - unlikely, but still possible
Universe! I asked for a beached, empty shell
You may have sent an intricate coral reef
And upon examination...no
Thank god! I humbly accept this gift.
An intricate shell at best!

Hot and cold
I've known you for years
But I didn't really know you
Never felt the desire to truly get to know you
Until now
Until that first hotel bar
That first glass of wine
I am seldom impressed or intrigued
You held my attention
Surprised me
Obsessively thought of me and felt sad when I said good night
Then the weather changed
Flashing hot to cold
In a weeks time
Obsession turned to disinterest
Not slowly, but within hours
Without warning
And so ended the fastest love in my life

If you fall in love with me
Don't
This is a reference to a lovely heartfelt poem
A spoken word poem I fell in love with once
I felt
Represented my heart once
Understood me once
But I can't take credit for
And let me tell you
Although heart ache, heart break, heart obsession, and heart devotion may have similar themes
Similar rhythms and patterns
No two loves are the same
So from here on
I will never type one letter, utter one word, or give one look to general love,
Because it is insulting to compare a Shakespeare sonnet
To any love - unknown

The middle road

◦ There is a middle road between societal success and disappointed expectation. why isnt it ok to be a mother and an mma fighter? A fitness liaison to a board of directors and an addict - a flawed force. Who decided what defined true self and life's meaning?

◦ I believe some karma is meant to serve the world - ripple the waters - but suffer the soul. Some karma - self understanding and molding. And still others, some of each depending on the moment

◦ Therefore find your calling - your true life's purpose - this life

◦ Embrace it and bow to it

Fuck her
She pretends to be spiritual, supportive
In my corner
But it's bullshit
She even might believe her bullshit
Talks about female power
Then posts herself in a bikini
Which is liked on social media
Copying my post a few months prior
And I'm jealous because hers is better
Sexier
I see how her subconscious intention was always to move me out
I allowed it
And I was ignorant
Fuck her

Gentle
There are loves who give - truly
Not by choice, but by gravity - unknown connection
Not bound by reason or practical thought
Drawn smoothly - mindlessly
And beautifully cradled
If you have never felt this, secure your judgement
Until you see and know something you love
Something that can't be unloved
We can't unknown what moves our souls

Don't touch me
My skin, my lips, space and presence
Every cell and follicle
They are mine - belong to me

Letting go
It gives us strength - self respect
Control and direction
And then a moment
A memory
Needles your heart
And begs to reconsider, to end the piercing that comes without warning or patterns
No predetermined frequency
Whispers in our ear that this pain is endless
To run back to what we know
Pathetic, begging, sacrificing, but familiar
Like a scalding bath we think will cool in time
We accept the burn, believing the water will soothe eventually
But we know this bath - this tub
It never changes
So eventually we have to leave again
This time for good, out the door
But cold prickles our wet skin - and the longing returns
With it the memories of warmth - not the burning
But this time we choose discomfort
We choose to shiver
And begin to find warmth - growing flame - within

Why don't I write about you?
You have been a corner stone.
And invaluable presence and teacher
The very reason for my demeanor and good fortune
I owe you everything. I can never repay you
And yet I don't write about you.
The oldest and deepest part of my heart holds your memories.
Like an antique keepsake or heirloom garden
Perhaps some loves - deep loves
Don't need words

I lost you
And it's as though you still exist
Because we talked, and made plans to visit
Discussed the weather - kids - politics

Women

These women - the very idea of them,

From the start- Innocent children - exploring

Limitless - unique goddess mold

Drawn to their talents - their purpose

But western culture meets with sharp judgment

What's 'ladylike' and expected

Suppression

Shame

Young women - starry eyed - hopeful

Eventually broken in

Boxed in - tamed with cinema storylines

Meant to be pleasing

Always apologizing

Apologizing for thinking

Apologizing for breathing

Apologizing for being

Enough!

'Sorry' should be reserved for remorse

Not authenticity

What we are
A woman being a woman
Hot, delicate, passionate, primal, aggressive, submissive-
Complex
Subdued in the sunlight
Reaching soul and heart like new branches
Fluttering eyes at partitions in the leaves
Like an unmanned kite
Wistfully dancing without direction
Quiet growth - silent growth
The trees - like their mothers - bare undisclosed burden

What she deserves
Compassion and kindness
Firm hugs and soft words
When I see her suffer, I wonder
What karmic price she is paying from past life
Because in this one
There is no action, thought, or demeanor
No score to settle or own up to
She is love and well meaning to her core
And the fact she doesn't see it
Remains humble - still spirit
Reinforces the brightness of her soul
I proudly call her friend

Foolish
You see it - I see it - ignored
Pieces making perfection - rise up
Tying rock to anxious energy
Sinking cut out shadows
Inner circle - connected - clings tightest
To that image - truly last to let go
Blindly follow and blush
Horse blinders, but not struggling
Resting at the base of a tree
Trusting stable roots
Ignorant pleading innocence
So foolish - to willing loves slave
Pathetic and yet soothing
Warrior preparing for battle
Then melting - warm bath
◦ Snake coiling - subservient to oboe sound,
◦ But at deepest marrow - disgust

Rosaline
We know nothing of anything until struck by fates grace
Love assumed - presumed.
Obsessed with limitations
Until we meet
And time passes
Nothing remains the same

Split
Lover - mother
Huntress and gentle touch
Warrior and servant
Humble and fierce
Temptress - maternal
Female Dichotomy
How to embody - embrace true nature
How to accept - without shame, guilt, or fear?

You're wrong - you're right
I want to text you so badly right now
Tell you I miss you
And you don't deserve me
I'm anxious for your thoughts
Where are you?
What do you think of me?
Would you let me let myself in
Take off my clothes
Crawl into bed
Would you roll away from me, or worse
Would you have company
You told me you wanted space
I gave you space
What hurts me most is
You didn't want me close again
I wasn't worth the judgment
The slight discomfort of chasing what we had
You'd rather be loved by false friends
Then love me

#26

A poem for you
This is the last one
And will be the most transparent one
Clearly written and intended for you
I told you once of a dream I had years ago
A dream that intrigued and led me to you
I was walking in a dimming night
It began to snow and I got lost
You found me
You found me
And for that I am grateful
But now let me go

Message to Dante

My angel - sweetest heart and kindest soul

These are not weaknesses

They are pure gifts

Surround yourself with true support and unwavering love

Don't let wolves into your flock disguised as sheep

Trust your feelings more than your thoughts

Your desire to help everyone is noble, but you must protect yourself before your give to others

This is not selfish - it's how you fuel your fire and heat your soul - to better serve the world

Hear my voice whisper rest and self care whenever you feel guilty about retreating to recharge

Wrap my words and memories around you like a blanket

Know I am always protecting you with my wings

Because I love you unconditionally - that can not change

And I hold you so you are never afraid to share your gifts

Delicate gifts that are your heavy karmic burden to give

This world needs you - and I wish I could carry it for you

I'm not afraid
I'm not afraid - I'm brave
But then brave is quick to save
Superhero's - cape and mask
Leading the charge - not knowing task
Knuckles on hips - proud chin in air
Symbol of safety - though unaware
Of purpose - save from comfort felt
Beacon - nightlight - fear slowly melts
One day - illusion
False safety - shell
The story unraveling - layers fell
Unveiling core - the condensed truth/trust
∘ When dust settles- the hero's US

Message to Gabriel

There was no question when you were created, developed, and born. They were all on your time. You have always decided your journey.

Such a strong will and pure emotions

But you could embrace them fully and let go seconds later

You attacked me like you clung to me - completely

From day one you smiled at my voice and face differently then others

Complete love is different than most loves

It accepts anger and aggression - disgust and anguish - because it always turns back to love

We were born to fight as we were born to love

My sweet Aries -

And although my star sign is Aquarius/Pisces, I have Aries rising

Embrace your passions - be true to yourself

Stand alone if necessary but never compromise

You were born to stand out

And I ask you to ground your brother

He will float away with all his goodness and sensitivity if someone doesn't pull him down

This world needs your unique raw qualities and his compassionate heart

Be his foundation and anchor

He will never trust the world to share his gifts without you

Awkward angel
I know what I am
Always have
An angel trying to squeeze in this body
Find footing, like tight wool soxes
Searching for flush toes and heel
But honestly, it's awkward
Not graceful like most images of wings and serene figures
My wings aren't broken
Or plucked off in an oil painting to convey some sense of martyr or romance
I have grace, poise, light step and gentle touch - and gentle heart
But look closely
My knees have bruises
I bite my chapped lips when nervous
Especially when it's silent
I scratch mosquito bites - even though some have long stopped itching
I cling to phrases and words that mean nothing, but provide closure or acknowledge general conversation
Yes, I am an angel,
But as my spirit wiggles into physical form,
A soft layer of discomfort and unnatural float in some hollow spaces
Like daylight attempting to burn off fog
Dense fog
I blush and kick at gravel

Printed in the United States
by Baker & Taylor Publisher Services